EVERYTHING I
KNOW

A Play in Two Acts

Jerry Mitchell

ISBN 978-1-63814-724-4 (Paperback)
ISBN 978-1-63814-725-1 (Digital)

Covenant Books, Inc.
11661 Hwy 707
Murrells Inlet, SC 29576
www.covenantbooks.com

For my father

FOREWORD

Jerry Mitchell and I developed a close friendship during the years that he attended Calvary Chapel in Houston, Texas. Over my years of pastoring, I've met few followers of Jesus that have a heart as big as Jerry's to see the lost sinner come to know Jesus. I remember during one of our frequent lunch meetings talking about a group of terrorists that I would have loved to have seen eradicated, Jerry voiced concern over their lost souls and how he'd be praying they'd find Christ. My first thought was, *Jerry should be the pastor!*

Everything I Know is a powerful Gospel presentation that uniquely demonstrates the essence of the truth that the human heart is a vacuum—created by God and for God. Most of us know someone like the main character, Dr. Kevin Miller, who filled his life with human achievement and worldly success, only to discover at the end—something was missing. It may even be that you are holding this play in your hands and you are that "someone."

Personally, I was deeply touched by act 2, scene 4. That is the scene where Dr. Miller writes the final entry in his book which is central to the play. I felt that what he wrote was both the perfect ending and the perfect beginning. I can't say any more without giving it away!

Everything I Know is a captivating play that masterfully exposes the dilemma of the human heart that doesn't have Christ living inside. It is my prayer that this play will reach countless people both in its public presentation and as a book—leading many into a personal and immensely fulfilling relationship with Jesus Christ.

J. D. Glasscock
Senior Pastor
Calvary Chapel Houston Metro

PREFACE

*E*verything I Know is a story about a quiet, thoughtful, and very educated college professor facing the most difficult and most frightening challenge of his life: terminal cancer. Apart from the obvious issues, his greatest concern is that all the knowledge he has spent his life collecting will be lost upon his death. His solution is a book titled *Everything I Know*. This play follows his journey as he searches for meaning in his life—and death. In that sense, it is the story of every man.

The idea for this play originated in the range of thoughts and emotions I experienced while watching my father slowly grow sicker from, and ultimately die of, cancer. It was unthinkable to me that the knowledge and wisdom of this man who had taught me how to ride a bike, to throw a baseball, to fly a kite, and so many other of the most important lessons of life could be lost to us in an instant. What lessons did his untimely passing leave untaught?

As a play, *Everything I Know* was originally intended for public performance; hopefully, publication in book form will expand its reach to those who might not otherwise ever see it performed. Questions suitable for contemplation or group discussion have been included in this edition. I pray that this book will be a blessing for every reader, inspiring hesitant evangelists to be more like Hope Weaver, and touching the hearts, minds, and consciences of those who have not yet put their trust in Jesus.

Jerry Mitchell
King of Prussia, Pennsylvania
August 13, 2020

CONTENTS

CAST OF CHARACTERS

Kevin Miller: A professor of history at a small Texas college. A devoted and hardworking scholar, he has dedicated his life to his work. He's shy, introverted, and a lifelong bachelor.

Brian Evans: Miller's friend and colleague. He also teaches history at the college. He is Miller's opposite—large, bold, loud, and very outgoing.

Hope Weaver: A middle-aged widow who works as a shorthand court reporter.

Offstage Voice: Miller's physician

Paramedic 1: A paramedic working on an emergency ambulance.

Paramedic 2: A second paramedic working on an emergency ambulance.

Scene: Kevin Miller's living room

Time: The holiday season

ACT 1

SCENE 1

Setting: *The stage is dark.*

At rise: *Miller is sitting center stage, facing the audience. He is lit by a single spotlight.*

MILLER. Cancer?!

OFFSTAGE VOICE. It's commonly called oat cell carcinoma. It's a small cell lung cancer.

MILLER, *obviously taken by surprise.* Cancer... So...what am I looking at? Surgery? Chemo?

OFFSTAGE VOICE, *clinically.* Dr. Miller, this particular kind of cancer is aggressive and is typically...not operable. That is...especially true...in a case such as yours because the disease has progressed to what we call the "extensive stage."

MILLER. Extensive?!

OFFSTAGE VOICE. I'm afraid the scans indicate it has already spread to your brain. That is almost certainly the cause of your headaches and dizziness.

MILLER. Not operable? My brain...(*Miller unconsciously reaches up and touches his head, then a sudden rush of recognition.*) Does that mean...?

OFFSTAGE VOICE. There are some treatment options. We could try a course of chemotherapy. We could try a targeted radiation therapy for the metastasis in your brain.

MILLER. What...what are my...chances?

OFFSTAGE VOICE. Dr. Miller, you're an educated man. I know you can go out and dig up a lot of information on the internet—some good, most not so good—so I'm going to be frank with you. The prognosis is not promising. Given the extent of the cancer, we may be able to extend your life with treatment. Maybe as much as twelve to eighteen months.

MILLER. A year! (*Softer*) A year? (*After a pause*) And without treatment?

OFFSTAGE VOICE. Four months. Maybe six.

MILLER. Wow... I don't know what to say... What do I do?

OFFSTAGE VOICE, *still clinical.* I'm very sorry, Dr. Miller. (*Voice begins fading*) Why don't you take a few days to consider your options? We can talk again in a week or so to—

(*Blackout*)

(*End of scene*)

SCENE 2

Setting: *Evening. The Tuesday before Thanksgiving. Miller's living room. It is a modestly appointed room. There is a sofa facing the audience, center stage. The most outstanding feature of the room is a row of overstuffed bookcases along the back wall. There is a chess set on one of the bookshelves. One bookcase has a cabinet at the bottom of it. Left of the sofa is a small dining-style table with two chairs. A glass water pitcher and two glasses are on the table. Right of the sofa is an end table with a lamp. The front door is stage right. There is a coat rack near the door. There is a fireplace on the opposite side of the room.*

At rise: *Miller is seated on the sofa, facing the audience. He has an open laptop computer on his lap, but he is staring into space.*

There is a loud knock on the door. Miller's expression does not change, and he does not move. Another knock, this time more insistent.

EVANS, *from outside the door.* Kevin, it's seven o'clock! It's Tuesday! And it's very cold out here!

Miller finally stirs. He checks his watch, closes the laptop, and walks to the door. Another insistent knock just as Miller opens the door. When Miller opens the door, Dr. Brian Evans bursts into the room.

EVANS, *removing his hat and coat.* I know you like your solitude Kevin, but a guy could freeze out there waiting on your doorstep. I moved to Texas to get away from this kind of weather. No fire? (*Gesturing to the fireplace.*) Fortunately, I brought something special to keep us warm. (*Evans retrieves a bottle from his coat pocket.*) It's the eighteen-year-old. The good stuff! And since it's Thanksgiving week…(*Evans pulls two large cigars from his other coat pocket.*) A pair of Churchills to go with it! Thank goodness for Tuesday nights! Helen won't let me smoke at home at all anymore. I guess that's why we play chess! (*As he speaks, Evans puts the whiskey and cigars on the table and retrieves a chess set from the bookcase, which he also puts on the table.*) Which color am I tonight? Eh… I don't remember…you take white.

Evans sits at the table and spins the board around so that he has the black pieces. Miller, still looking dazed, sits across from him. Evans pours two generous glasses of whiskey using the glasses on the table, and raises his as if for a toast.

EVANS. Death to the enemy!

Miller unenthusiastically raises his glass and clinks Evans's. Evans takes a long drink. Miller does not; he simply puts his glass back down.

EVANS. Okay! Your move!

The men begin to play chess. Evans talks throughout.

EVANS. If it's actually going to get this cold, I'm going to need a thicker coat. We may have to close the college and cancel classes in the morning if the roads ice. Makes no sense to me though. We cancel classes to keep the kids off the roads and all they'll do is get on the roads to get a head start home for the holiday. They'd probably be safer in class. You have your final ready? I'm way behind on it myself. I'll probably spend part of the weekend preparing it. I thought about using last year's, but I think the kids are on to me. I don't want to be an easy "A," you know? (*Evans drains his glass and picks up the bottle to refill it.*) You haven't touched your scotch! It's the good stuff…the eighteen.

If you're not careful, I'll drink it all. Ah…maybe that's your cunning plan…

Miller makes a very bad move, resulting in the loss of his queen. For the first time all evening, Evans actually looks at his friend.

EVANS. Everything okay, Kevin? You don't seem yourself. You're not trying to let me win, are you?

Miller has a short but intense and obviously painful coughing fit. He holds a handkerchief to his mouth as he coughs.

EVANS. That's not getting any better. Maybe you should break down and see a doctor.

MILLER. I did.

Evans picks up the cigars and tries to hand one to Miller, who waves it away.

EVANS, *while clipping the end of his cigar.* What did he say? Sounds to me like you could have walking pneumonia.

MILLER. No, fortunately I do *not* have pneumonia. (*A brief pause as Miller swallows hard; this is the first time he has said it out loud.*) He said I have inoperable lung cancer that has spread to my brain.

The men look at each other silently for a moment. Evans puts his cigar down.

EVANS. You're not joking…

MILLER. The joke is on me, actually. I have oat cell carcinoma. I'm dying. It's just a matter of how long.

Evans is uncharacteristically at a loss for words. He opens his mouth to say something, but nothing comes out.

MILLER. It's true. I am going to die. If I do chemo, I may have a year and a half, but I've been reading up on it. The side effects sound like it would be one very miserable year and a half. But if I don't do it I've only got about six months. Maybe four...

Evans opens his mouth to respond again, but still nothing comes out.

MILLER. So which do I choose? The long slow painful death? Or the even longer, slower, more painful death?

EVANS, *obviously stunned.* Kevin... I...

Miller coughs again. Evans picks up the cigars and moves them toward his pocket.

EVANS. We certainly don't need these...

MILLER, *with an ironic smile.* I'm dying. What's a cigar going to do? Kill me? (*Miller drains his glass of whiskey.*) And a refill, barkeep! (*Miller gestures to Evans to hand him a cigar.*)

EVANS. I'm not sure that would be a good idea. Neither is the whiskey. (*Evans picks up the bottle and puts it in his jacket pocket.*) I'm really sorry...

MILLER. I don't have many friends, Brian. Heck, who am I kidding? You are my only friend. Please don't go weird on me.

EVANS. Maybe I should go... You probably need to rest...

Evans gets up and begins to move toward the coat rack.

MILLER, *insistently*. Actually, I wish you would stay. I really need to talk.

Evans sits back down, but he is clearly very uncomfortable.

MILLER. I'm scared, Brian. I'm afraid of dying. I'm afraid of one day just not being able to breathe. I'm afraid of the pain. It's in my brain too. I'm afraid I'll wake up one day and not remember who I am. But do you know what I'm most afraid of?

Evans shakes his head no. He is in shock but is now determined to be strong for his friend.

MILLER. When I'm gone, there will be nothing left to prove I was ever even here. No wife. No children. No legacy. All I've ever done is spend my life filling my brain with knowledge. I study and teach history. That's it. Names. Dates. Battles. Kings. Learning them has been my life's work. I realized today that the moment I die, all that work, all that learning, all that knowledge…will be lost. Forever. That's what scares me the most.

A brief silence, during which Evans puts his cigar in his mouth and starts chewing it thoughtfully without lighting it.

EVANS. Then you need to preserve it. Save all that stuff in your brain for future generations.

MILLER, *not taking Evans seriously*. Preserve it? Put my head in a jar like some late-night sci-fi movie or something?

EVANS. No. Put your knowledge on paper. Or at least in a computer. Record it on tape. Any of those could keep all of that stuff in your head alive forever.

MILLER, *frowns skeptically but then decides to grasp at this straw of hope.* Actually… I could do that. I could write down everything I've learned…or at least as much as I…can. Brian, you are a genius.

EVANS. I've always thought so. Put it all in a book (*gesturing grandly*). You can call it *Everything I Know.*

MILLER. No one would ever really want to read it, of course, but at least I could… There's just so little time…

EVANS. The semester is almost over. I can take over your classes. They meet, what, three, four more times before the final? I'll call Dean Wolters in the morning. That would free you up to work on this book project.

MILLER. But you know what a poor typist I am. I'd have to hire a typist… Do typists still take shorthand?

EVANS. Shorthand… Why don't you hire one of those shorthand court reporters who type everything lawyers say in court? You could just talk as fast as you want to, and the court reporter would get it all down for you.

MILLER. Even better! How do you hire one of those?

EVANS. There have to be agencies. We could look one up online.

MILLER, *energized for the first time, moves to get his laptop.* I'm going to look right now.

Miller opens the laptop, and the two men hover over it as Miller types in search terms.

EVANS. Just type in "shorthand court reporting services." How much do you think they cost? Man, this was a good idea!

MILLER. Here we go. We've got several to choose from.

Miller and Evans ad lib about cost, options, etc.

(Blackout)

(End of scene)

SCENE 3

Setting: *Late morning. Miller's living room.*

At rise: *Miller is seated at the table across from a pleasant middle-aged woman, Hope Weaver. Weaver has a bag containing a stenography machine sitting beside her. She is dressed professionally in a wintry suit. Her winter coat hangs on the coat rack. She is listening intently to Miller.*

MILLER. I really appreciate you being able to come on such short notice, especially with the holiday tomorrow.

WEAVER. No problem at all, Dr. Miller. I was told you needed someone right away.

MILLER. I've never worked with a court reporter before, so please excuse me if I don't understand quite how your job works. I'm not a lawyer and I'm not involved in a lawsuit.

WEAVER. Okay.

MILLER. I'm writing a book.

WEAVER. A book!

MILLER. And it's not your typical book, I'm afraid. As I told your agency, I am a professor of history at the college. I typically teach European history, though I have also taught overview classes to underclassmen. This may sound strange, but my goal is to make a record of everything I've learned. In fact, I'm calling it *Everything I Know*.

WEAVER. What a great name! Will there be a particular country or time or king that you are going to write about?

MILLER. No, Ms. Weaver. I literally want us to put on paper *everything* I know.

WEAVER. Oh…

MILLER. I would like to dictate and have you record and transcribe my dictation. Then I would like you to produce hard copy drafts that I can review and edit. I need to finish it as quickly as possible, so I'd like to try to dictate all day and get the drafts from the previous day each morning. I realize that will be a burden on you, but I'm afraid it can't be helped. I am working on, well, let's just call it a hard deadline. Do you think you can help me?

WEAVER, *shaking her head*. Well, that's a new one for me. I've never worked on a book before. And *everything*, you know? An educated man like you? How long do you think that's going to take?

MILLER. I'm told four to six months, maybe a little less. As I said, it's a hard deadline. I know I am essentially asking you to work day and night. Rest assured, I will be doing the same. Do you have a husband or a family that you need to care for in the evenings?

WEAVER. Not anymore, Doctor. My dear Arthur passed away six years ago, and my son, Thomas, is grown now. It's just me. But you are describing a pretty tough schedule. Are you thinking about working at that pace all five days a week?

MILLER. I was actually thinking seven…but I suppose I can compromise, and perhaps we could agree on a daily schedule that would permit you to get started on the day's transcription before it gets late. We could, say, dictate new material from eight to four each day, then you could work on the drafts after that, either here or at your home, whichever you prefer.

WEAVER. We normally work five days a week. I'll definitely need Sundays off, but I am not afraid of hard work, Doctor. I am willing to try Monday through Saturday if it's really that urgent. Did you talk to the agency about the schedule? Did you work out pricing for all of that?

MILLER. The charges are taken care of. We can start out working Monday through Saturday. If that is too much, we can make adjustments. In addition, I know there will be days when I will have other…appointments that I need to attend.

WEAVER. I presume we would take tomorrow off?

MILLER. Tomorrow?

WEAVER. Thanksgiving?

MILLER. Oh yes. Of course (*smiles*). So do we have a deal?

WEAVER, *smiles broadly*. Actually, I think it sounds exciting! And certainly different. When do we start?

MILLER. The sooner the better. Today if you can. I see you have a bag. Did you bring your equipment?

WEAVER. I've got everything I need right here. I can set up in just a few minutes. (*Weaver begins assembling her stenographic machine.*)

MILLER. Excellent! Then let's start now. (*Miller jumps up and moves to the cupboard.*) Can I get you a glass of water or something else to drink? It's still a little before noon, but a friend left me an excellent bottle of scotch…

WEAVER. No, thank you. I don't drink. Water will be just fine.

Miller pours a glass of water from a pitcher on the table and puts it in front of Weaver.

WEAVER. Thank you.

Miller picks up a legal pad that has notes scrawled on multiple pages and begins flipping through the pages.

WEAVER. So how long have you been teaching at the college?

MILLER, *still reviewing notes on the pad.* A long time. I started teaching while I was working on my doctorate. When I finished my PhD, they offered me a tenure track position. (*Miller puts the notes down on the table and is serious for a moment.*) It was all I ever wanted…

WEAVER. I never went to college myself. I always wanted to. I always meant to. I guess the time was never right. I got married, had my son. It all happens so fast—

Weaver is cut off by Miller having a coughing fit. He turns away so she won't see the blood on his handkerchief.

WEAVER. Are you all right?

MILLER. Yes. Yes I am. Just a bit of a cough.

WEAVER. That was more than a bit, I'd say. Are you sure you're okay?

MILLER, *smiling.* Much better. Now, Mrs. Weaver, I think you're about to get some education in history at the very least.

Weaver, *visibly relaxing from her alarm.* I'm ready. I would've loved to study history. All those stories about interesting people…

MILLER. Good. Well... I guess I'll just start. If you can't understand me or I go too fast just let me know, okay?

Weaver nods and assumes a typing posture. She begins typing when Miller begins speaking.

MILLER. I apologize that this may seem disjointed and disorganized at times, but... Ms. Weaver?

WEAVER, *stops typing and looks up at Miller*. Yes?

MILLER. We hadn't started yet. You needn't record my apology for the lack of organization...

WEAVER. Sorry. Just tell me when to start.

MILLER, *hangs his head and smiles*. I was just warning you that I am not going to start at the beginning. I think I should begin in the areas where my knowledge is strongest, then fill in the rest later.

WEAVER. Yes, sir. I'm not sure I would have noticed.

MILLER. Okay. Let's begin with the Norman invasion of England in 1066. Maybe you should put that as a heading or chapter or whatever.

Weaver complies.

MILLER. And...begin.

Weaver begins typing. Miller paces back and forth across the room as he dictates.

MILLER. *Everything I Know*, volume 1. The Norman invasion of England, AD 1066. The Normans invaded, conquered, and occupied England in the AD eleventh century. The invasion commenced in 1066 following the death of King Edward the Confessor of England and the dynastic struggle occasioned by his death. The key player in the Norman Conquest was William I, Duke of Normandy, also known as William the Conqueror. He was born out of wedlock to his father Robert I, Duke of Normandy, and his mistress, Herleva, in approximately 1028. Unfortunately, the exact date of his birth cannot be verified.

(Lights begin fading.)

MILLER. Despite his illegitimacy, William succeeded his father as duke and, later, as a potential heir to the English throne through his cousin, Edward the Confessor, who had no children...

(Blackout)

(End of scene)

SCENE 4

Setting: *Miller's living room. Late afternoon. There is now a stack of transcripts on the table.*

At rise: *Weaver is packing up her equipment. Miller is sitting in a chair rubbing his eyes.*

Miller gets up, walks to the end table, and retrieves a mobile phone. He calls a number and puts the phone to his ear.

MILLER, *on the phone.* Brian? Yes. I'm okay. A little tired. Yes, I guess so. Listen, I know it's Tuesday, but I really need to work on the book tonight. I know… I know… I know it is the highlight of your week. Wait, now that's a little melodramatic, don't you think? You're right. I probably do need a break. No I didn't just change my mind… Brian, I'm sorry, but please listen… You know how important this is to me. And I have so little time… Thank you for understanding. Why don't you go to a cigar bar to smoke? I know it's not the same… I would hope it's not the same…okay. I'll check in with you tomorrow… Okay… Good… Yes…yes… Okay… Goodbye.

Miller hangs up the phone and sighs out loud.

MILLER. I'm sorry about that, Ms. Weaver. I just needed to make a quick call before I get tied up in revising and organizing yesterday's draft.

WEAVER. I couldn't help overhearing, and please forgive me if it's none of my business, but did you have something planned for this evening?

MILLER. Yes. My weekly chess date with a friend.

WEAVER. As I said, it's none of my business, but you've been working awfully hard these last two weeks, and you seem exhausted. Maybe a night off with your friend would do you some good.

MILLER. It is not your business, and there just isn't enough time.

Massaging his temples and rubbing his eyes, Miller sits down heavily on the sofa and has an obviously painful coughing fit.

WEAVER. Dr. Miller! Are you okay? (*Weaver moves to the sofa to check on Miller.*)

MILLER. I'm fine. Let me catch my breath, and I'll be fine.

Miller is obviously not fine. Weaver can see his handkerchief is spotted with blood.

WEAVER. Should I call 911? (*Weaver moves toward her bag.*)

MILLER. I said *I'm fine!*

This sets off another coughing fit. Weaver reaches into her bag and retrieves a cell phone.

WEAVER. I'm calling! (*Weaver starts to call.*)

MILLER, *more calmly.* Please don't.

Weaver hesitates.

MILLER. They can't help me. They'll just want to put me in some hospice where I won't—

Miller cuts off abruptly, realizing he said too much.

WEAVER, *puts down her phone.* Hospice? That's why all of this is such a big hurry, isn't it?

MILLER, *with resignation.* Yes. Yes, it is.

Weaver pours a glass of water and brings it to Miller.

MILLER. Thank you. (*Miller gives a weak smile.*)

WEAVER. May I ask what's wrong?

Miller grimaces and then hangs his head a moment before answering.

MILLER. I have terminal cancer. I have decided against treatments that might have extended my life by a year or so. I've got maybe three to six months left.

WEAVER. I'm so very sorry. (*Weaver sits beside Miller.*) Maybe we should slow down our pace. I know I'm worn out. I can't imagine—

MILLER. No. I won't be able to really explain this to you, but I *need* to work on the book. I *need* the reason to get out of bed every morning. I *need* to create something that will survive after I'm gone. It's my only chance for…immortality.

WEAVER. Dr. Miller, I'm sorry, but I have to disagree.

Miller looks over at Weaver with a mix of irritation and curiosity.

MILLER. Oh?

WEAVER. You *are* immortal. We all are. Our loving Creator made us that way. We are all going to live forever.

MILLER, *mockingly.* Forever? I wish you'd tell my doctor that because he seems to disagree.

WEAVER, *scolding him.* Your eternal destiny is not a joke. You are going to live forever. (*Softer*) The only question is where. God made us eternal beings. He wants us to choose to spend that eternity with Him.

MILLER. How do you even know there really is a God?

WEAVER. That's a very big question. The real answer is that I know He exists because of faith and because of His truth revealed in the Bible. But I know that's not the answer you're looking for.

MILLER. So He exists because you believe He does?

WEAVER. No. He exists whether you or I believe it or not. Let's take just one part of who God is—the Creator.

MILLER, *skeptically.* Okay…

WEAVER. Do you see that painting over your fireplace? Did that just spring into being, or was there a painter who created it?

MILLER. Of course, someone painted it.

WEAVER. So we know there was a painter because the painting exists. The same with this apartment building. Did it just randomly appear as the result of cosmic dust falling just right, or was there a builder who carefully planned and constructed it?

MILLER. Someone built it, obviously.

WEAVER. That's right. We know there was a builder because the building exists. So think about all of the wonders of this earth—all the people, the animals and the plants, the atmosphere, the mountains. Is it so much easier to see that a simple painting required a painter than it is to see that all the wonders of the universe required a creator? It didn't happen by chance any more than that painting. (*Weaver points to the painting.*) The fact that we, the earth, and the universe exist proves He exists.

Weaver and Miller sit quietly a moment while Miller digests this perspective he's never heard before.

WEAVER. Have you thought about what happens after we die?

MILLER. Almost constantly these days. I think probably nothing. I think...we're just...gone. I wish I could believe in a place like heaven, but I just don't see it.

WEAVER, *puts her hand on his shoulder and makes hard eye contact.* Heaven is very real, Dr. Miller. Unfortunately, so is hell. God wants you to spend eternity in heaven with Him, but you get to choose. Do you know where you are going to spend your eternity?

MILLER. Probably in an urn...

Weaver cocks her head and frowns at Miller. He shrugs his shoulders and continues.

MILLER. If there is a God, I'm sure He knows I am a pretty good person. At least I try to be. I've never murdered anyone. I've never robbed a bank. I mean... I know I'm not perfect, but there are a lot of people a lot worse than me. Plus He's supposed to be all loving and merciful, right? If there were a heaven, I think I am good enough to get in.

WEAVER, *shaking her head.* I'm afraid it doesn't work like that. We all break God's laws, even the so-called good people among us. You, me, all of us. We have all sinned and fallen short of God's Holy perfection. That makes all of us guilty and unworthy to stand in God's presence.

MILLER, *incredulous.* What! So now you're telling me there's no hope?

Weaver begins shaking her head and trying to interrupt, but Miller keeps talking.

MILLER. Are you saying there is a loving God who wants to spend eternity with us, but we can't go to heaven because we're not absolutely perfect, so instead we are all going to hell...that... that I'm going to hell!

WEAVER. No, sir. I'm not. I said we all deserve hell. But God, in His mercy, gave us a way to be saved from hell. Do you know what He did?

MILLER, *still skeptical, but he really wants to hear this.* No...

WEAVER, *boldly.* Our magnificent God sent His only Son, Jesus Christ, to earth to become a man, to suffer and die, and to pour out His precious blood as a sacrifice. He took the punishment for my sins. And for yours too. All you have to do is accept this precious gift He offers you. (*Weaver wipes a tear from her eye.*)

MILLER. You're saying that just because Jesus died for my sins, I can go to heaven?

WEAVER. Isn't it marvelous? All you have to do is say yes. Just acknowledge and repent of your sins, ask for His forgiveness, and thank Him for taking your punishment.

MILLER. Interesting...(*Skeptical again*) That's it? Really?

WEAVER. That's it! I'll be praying for you, Dr. Miller. Jesus wants you. Accept His mercy and grace. (*Weaver gets up, wiping her eyes, and begins to collect her things.*)

MILLER. Ms. Weaver…

WEAVER. Please, call me Hope.

MILLER. Hope, thank you for sharing your beliefs with me. I'm a very private person, and I don't have a lot of unguarded moments with other people. So…just…thank you. You've given me some things to think about.

WEAVER. Good night, Dr. Miller. Get some rest. I'll see you tomorrow.

Weaver turns to leave. As she gets to the door, Miller calls out.

MILLER. Ms. Weaver…

WEAVER. Hope.

MILLER. Hope…where did you learn all that stuff? You know…the painter and the builder?

WEAVER. I never did tell you about my Arthur, did I? Well, let's just say I was a preacher's wife for thirty-two years. I've heard a lot of good sermons. Good night now.

Weaver walks off. Miller sits at the table and begins to work on the stack of transcripts. After a moment, he puts down his pen, rubs his eyes, leans back thoughtfully, and looks at the painting.

(*Blackout*)

(*End of scene*)

SCENE 5

Setting: *Afternoon. Miller's living room. The stack of transcripts on the table is noticeably higher.*

At rise: *Miller is pacing back and forth, dictating. Weaver is typing on her stenographic machine.*

MILLER. Tiglath-Pileser continued these reforms of Assyrian society throughout his reign. Indeed, his reforms were so sweeping that historians frequently mark his reign as the beginning of the Second Assyrian Empire. He was succeeded by his son Shalmaneser... V, I believe, who continued his father's expansion of the empire through military conquest. He was killed during a siege of Samaria and was succeeded by the commander of his army, who took the name Sargon as king—(*Miller is interrupted by a coughing fit.*) Let's take a little break.

Weaver stops typing and gets up to stretch while Miller drains a glass of water. Miller then sits on the sofa and rubs his eyes and temples. Weaver breaks the silence.

WEAVER. Are you doing anything special for Christmas, Dr. Miller?

MILLER. No... I guess not. I don't have any close family, so I generally don't make a fuss about it. (*A thoughtful pause.*) I hadn't really thought about it, but...maybe I should do something. This could be...

WEAVER. Well, my son and his wife and daughters are coming to visit me for the holiday. We would love to have you join us for Christmas dinner.

MILLER. I couldn't intrude on your family time like that.

WEAVER. No intrusion at all! I insist.

MILLER, *genuinely touched but not sure that's such a good idea.* I will definitely think about it, Hope. Thank you for inviting me. So shall we get back to work?

Weaver returns to her seat and assumes her typing position.

MILLER. Ready?

Weaver nods.

MILLER. Where did I leave off?

Weaver scrolls on her machine.

WEAVER. Sargon just became king.

MILLER. Thank you (*resumes pacing*). Sargon became king in approximately 720 BC. During his reign, Sargon's main rival for primacy in the region was Egypt, which set out to incite rebellion among Assyria's vassal states. When the Egyptians formed an alliance with some of his subjected peoples, Sargon went to war against Egypt's new allies, including the kingdom of Judah. He led his army on a march of conquest toward Jerusalem, destroying cities and towns as he went. He arrived at the city of Jerusalem and prepared a siege, but after he suffered a major defeat and lost nearly two hundred thousand men, he abandoned the siege and returned to Nineveh—

WEAVER. Dr. Miller?

MILLER. Yes?

WEAVER. I'm really sorry, but I think there may be a mistake.

MILLER, *surprised*. A mistake?

WEAVER. Yes, sir. I'm sorry, but I know this story…

MILLER, *skeptically*. Really?

WEAVER. Yes, sir. The story of the Assyrian king who attacked Jerusalem and had his army destroyed in one night.

MILLER. Yes, Sargon. I was just dictating that.

WEAVER. I think that his name was actually Sennacherib.

MILLER. Sennacherib?

WEAVER. Yes.

MILLER. Well, Ms. Weaver, I recall you saying how much you enjoyed your history classes in high school, but I'm the one with a PhD in history who has been teaching history in college for nearly three decades. I'm pretty sure I know what I'm talking about.

WEAVER. I really don't mean any disrespect. I just thought you'd want it to be right…

MILLER, *with a haughty tone*. Ha! Right, indeed! Well, I don't want you to feel we're making a mistake. I happen to have an excellent volume on the Second Assyrian Empire. (*Miller moves to the shelf and looks for a book.*) That should be able to bring you some comfort. (*Miller pulls a particular book from the shelf.*)

Ah! Here we go! (*Miller turns to the index in the back of the book.*) Let's see…siege of Jerusalem…page 236. (*Miller flips to a page in the middle of the book and starts reading.*) In 701 BC, Sennach—(*Miller stops midword, both shocked and embarrassed.*) Sennacherib…you were right.

WEAVER. I'm sorry, Dr. Miller. I shouldn't have said anything.

MILLER, *putting the book away.* No. No. You…did the right thing. I do want it to be correct. (*Miller sits on the sofa and touches his hands to his head.*) Is it happening already?

WEAVER. Is what happening?

MILLER. Nothing. (*Miller gets up and moves to the table.*) May I ask… how do you know about Sennacherib?

WEAVER. I was a pastor's wife for thirty-two years, remember? (*Weaver reaches into her bag and pulls out a well-worn Bible.*) It's all in here.

MILLER, *surprised.* In the Bible?

WEAVER. In fact, I think it's in here three times. (*Weaver turns to 2 Kings chapter 18.*) You see, the story of Sennacherib starts here in the eighteenth chapter of the book of Second Kings, and it goes over to chapter 19, where it says, "That night the angel of the LORD went out to the Assyrian camp and killed 185,000 Assyrian soldiers. When the surviving Assyrians woke up the next morning, they found corpses everywhere. Then King Sennacherib of Assyria broke camp and returned to his own land."

Miller reads over Weaver's shoulder. She holds up the Bible for him to see.

MILLER. Hmm...well... Sargon II was also a king of the Second Assyrian Empire. I'm certain of that. Is he in there as well?

WEAVER. In the book of Isaiah, I believe. Isaiah was a prophet of God who lived during the reigns of both Sargon and Sennacherib.

Miller, *still reading over Weaver's shoulder*. Interesting... And that's all...in there?

WEAVER. M-hmm. There are lots of great kings in here. Nebuchadnezzar, king of Babylon. King Cyrus of Persia...

MILLER. I didn't realize...and you learned all of that from...the Bible?

WEAVER. God's Word is a treasure trove.

MILLER. Mrs.—(*Miller catches Weaver's sidelong glance and stops himself.*) Hope. I'm sorry, but I'm very tired, and my head is aching. Can we stop a little early today?

WEAVER. Of course. You need to take care of yourself. (*Weaver starts packing her things.*) You let me know about Christmas dinner though. I really would like you to come.

MILLER, *with a hand to his head*. Do you mind letting yourself out today? I'm going to go and get some Tylenol for this headache. Tomorrow is Christmas Eve. You should take the day off. I'm sure you've got a lot to do to prepare for your family's visit.

WEAVER. I do! Thank you, sir. Don't you have anything stronger than Tylenol?

MILLER, *still rubbing his head*. I have a prescription, but I only take it when I need to sleep. I want to think clearly...at least as long as I can.

WEAVER. Please get some rest.

Miller nods and starts to walk off, but stops and turns around. Weaver is still packing.

MILLER, *with genuine humility.* Hope, I'm very sorry that I doubted that you knew what you were talking about. Obviously, I still have a lot to learn.

Miller turns and continues off.

WEAVER, *smiling.* You don't owe me any apologies, Doctor.

Weaver continues packing. The last item left unpacked is her Bible. She picks it up, but as she is about to put it in her bag, she stops. She turns and looks in the direction Miller just exited. She looks heavenward, mutters a short prayer, and puts the Bible lovingly on the table. She closes her bag and exits. As the door closes, Miller returns. He sees the Bible and, thinking it was accidentally forgotten, picks it up, runs to the door, opens it, and looks out. He doesn't see her, so he closes the door and stands looking at the Bible. Then he takes a seat at the table, pushes aside a stack of transcripts, and begins reading at the beginning.)

MILLER. Genesis, chapter 1. "In the beginning God created the heavens and the earth…"

(*Blackout*)

(*End of act*)

ACT 2

SCENE 1

Setting: *Miller's living room. Early evening.*

At rise: *Miller is sitting at the table reading Weaver's Bible.*

Miller periodically pauses from his reading to scribble notes on his yellow notepad. A loud knock on the door.

EVANS, *from outside the door.* Kevin, open up…it's Santa's elf!

His concentration broken, Miller looks up and smiles. He gets up, closes the Bible, looks around, and moves the Bible and his notepad to the side table near the lamp. Then he goes and opens the door. Evans bursts into the room with his customary energy. Evans is carrying a wrapped Christmas package and a paper grocery bag in one hand and a small decorated Christmas tree in the other. He is wearing a ridiculous elf hat.

EVANS. Merry Christmas, Kevin! I know it's not Tuesday, but we've missed a few chess nights, and it's Christmas Eve and all, so I thought I'd pop in and bring you some Christmas cheer. Where can I plug this in?

Evans holds out the tree.

MILLER, *laughing in spite of himself.* Look, it's the biggest elf in the North Pole!

Miller takes the little tree and sets it on the table while Evans takes off his coat and hangs it up. Evans keeps the elf hat on.

EVANS. Hey, if Santa had more elves my size, he'd get all of his toys finished by July each year.

MILLER. Yes, but his grocery budget would bankrupt the whole operation!

EVANS. Indeed! This is for you, my dear friend. (*Evans hands the package to Miller.*) It's not much, but I think you'll like it. Go ahead, open it!

MILLER, *sincerely moved.* Brian, you shouldn't have. I'm afraid I didn't get you anything.

EVANS. You can give me an autographed copy of your book. Do you still have that bottle of scotch? (*Evans goes to the shelf, retrieves the bottle of Scotch, moves the bottle to the table, and pours himself a glass while he continues talking.*) Maybe time for one quick game of chess? I need to watch the clock, though. If I'm late for another one of the kids' school pageants, I'll be sleeping on your couch. Go ahead and open it because I've brought other goodies too.

Evans holds up the grocery bag.

MILLER, *grinning.* Okay. (*Miller begins unwrapping the gift but stops to look at Evans.*) Now, Brian, you're not serious about an autographed copy, are you? You realize *Everything I Know* isn't really for publication, right?

EVANS. Who knows? I promise to read it at the very least. I've long wondered what was going on in the dark recesses of that introverted mind of yours. This book may be my best chance! (*Evans drains his glass and pours another.*) Can I pour you one or are you sticking to the diet even on Christmas Eve?

MILLER. I'm trying to follow the diet. It's amazing what a motivator the threat of imminent death can be…for all sorts of things…

EVANS. Then I won't feel bad about having another. Now, are you going to open that gift, or do I have to do it for you? I'm dying to see what you think!

MILLER. Okay, okay. (*Miller opens the package. It is a very old book.*) *African Game Trails*... Theodore Roosevelt. This cover, it looks like the first edition.

Miller flips to the title page to confirm.

EVANS. First edition, all right! And look at the leaf.

Miller complies. His eyes grow wide, and his mouth drops open.

EVANS. Yup! Signed by your favorite president himself! (*Evans beams with pride at the special gift.*)

MILLER. Brian, I'm blown away. This...this is a treasure. How did you find it? It must have cost a small fortune!

EVANS. Hey now, it's not polite to ask those kinds of questions about a Christmas gift. Besides, didn't I say I was Santa's elf? I even have the hat (*gestures*). Oh, and now for the other goodies! (*Evans pulls a bottle of white liquid from the bag.*) Sugar-free eggnog! (*Evans pulls a tin with a cake in it from the bag.*) And... Helen baked you an almond-flour cake! Personally, I think it tastes horrible, but Helen says it's okay for your diet, and everyone should have cake for Christmas!

MILLER. You guys are so great. Please give Helen a thank-you kiss for me.

EVANS. I will. How about that game of chess? (*Evans moves to retrieve the chess set, but the table is covered with manuscripts except for where Miller was reading Weaver's Bible.*) Kevin, can you just clear some of that away so I can put this board down?

MILLER, *snapping out of a trance as he admires his Roosevelt book*. Yeah, sure, of course.

Miller begins stacking some transcript papers and moves them to the side table.

EVANS, *setting the board down*. So how is the book coming? You certainly seem to be making great progress based on the volume of papers...

Miller is making room for his stacks on the side table, pushing the lamp and the Bible aside. The Bible and his notes fall on the floor. Evans springs to the rescue.)

EVANS. Whoa, let me help you with that. (*Evans picks up the Bible and looks it over, perplexed.*) Yours?

MILLER, *uncomfortably*. It belongs to Ho—to Ms. Weaver, the woman who is helping me with the book. She left it here yesterday.

EVANS, *handing the Bible to Miller*. Bible thumper, huh? (*Shaking his head*) I can only imagine the refuse she's dishing out to you, especially with your...sorry, Kevin.

MILLER. Have you ever read it?

EVANS. What, the Bible?

MILLER. Yes.

EVANS, *returns to his scotch*. I've read bits and pieces over the years, I suppose. I have not read the whole thing, no. Why, have you?

MILLER. I guess, just like you, I had read or heard bits and pieces at funerals or weddings, but I'd never studied it. Yesterday, I learned that there is a lot of good history recorded in here.

(*Miller gestures with the Bible.*) And after Hope left it here, I just got this sudden urge to pick it up and read it. I started at the beginning, in Genesis, and once I started, I couldn't put it down. I've got a lot of questions. I've even been taking notes. (*Miller picks up the notepad and gestures with it.*)

EVANS, *confused*. Questions? Notes?

MILLER. Yeah. Things that don't make sense to me or that probably need more background explanation. There are some good footnotes in there, but I'm still lost on some of it. Like I said though, I can't stop reading it. I stayed up almost all night. I was still reading it when you arrived this evening.

EVANS. Why the sudden interest? I never knew you were religious.

MILLER. I'm not, but, Brian, I hope you can understand that I've been thinking a lot about what happens after we...about what is going to happen after I...die. I just have this feeling pounding in my head that the answer to that question...just might be...in here.

Miller gestures with the Bible. Evans pulls a cigar from his jacket pocket and puts it in his mouth.

EVANS. Don't worry. I'm not going to light it. It just helps me to think if I chew on it.

MILLER. So what do you think happens after a person dies?

EVANS. Kevin, are you sure you really want to talk about this?

MILLER. I *have* to talk about this. Can't you see that?

EVANS. Do you really want my honest thoughts?

MILLER. Of course. I value your opinions, and I certainly didn't ask you the question to solicit a lie.

EVANS. Kevin, I really don't want to get in the way of whatever comfort you are taking from exploring this Bible thing. I know what you're going through must be terrifying, and if I were in your shoes, I'd probably crawl into a fetal position and stay there. But since you asked, I will give you my best answer.

MILLER. Please do.

EVANS, *assumes his professorial tone.* I think, based on my decades of study, that individuals in every human civilization since the beginning have struggled with an inability to intellectually cope with the concept of their own non-existence. That struggle has made the fear of death a universal human experience. In virtually every society throughout history, the way people have resolved that fear has been to construct a religious system with a deity or deities—be it Zeus, Ra, Odin, Allah, Vishnu or, dare I say... Jehovah—something bigger than themselves that is in control and is protecting them. And all of those religious systems include some conceptualization of an afterlife, be that reincarnation, heaven, Elysium, Valhalla, or whatever. Unfortunately, each of those concepts is the product of the imaginations of frightened men, and nothing more. I'm sorry, Kevin, but that's how I see it. (*Evans pours himself another scotch.*) As I said though, I truly don't want to tell you what to believe. (*Evans swallows the glass of scotch.*)

MILLER. Don't worry, Brian, you haven't offended me. I've always seen it that way too. But now...now I'm just not so sure. There is some truth in this book. (*Miller is still holding the Bible and holds it up.*)

EVANS, *shaking his head.* There are also a lot of errors and contradictions.

MILLER. Maybe...but, Brian, twenty-four hours ago, I had a high school-educated, middle-aged widow correcting me on ancient history just because she'd read about it in here. (*Miller gestures with the Bible again.*)

EVANS. Do a Google search. You'll see what I mean. For example, Richard Dawkins points out that based on the timeline of the purported events in the Bible, the Earth would only be about six thousand years old. You're a historian, man. You know that human civilization goes back many times longer than that based on radiocarbon dating of artifacts. And geologists date the earth at, what...thirteen billion years old or something like that? The Bible simply can't be reconciled with science.

MILLER. I will Google it. And I will keep studying it. Like I said, I can't stop. But can I share with you some things I've been contemplating?

EVANS. Yeah...sure...

MILLER. When we put our trust in man-made science like radiocarbon dating or the big bang or evolution, theories that can't truly be proven by testing or experimentation, is that really any less an act of "faith" than trusting the Bible? I mean...maybe it all really just comes down to whether we choose to place our faith in God or in men...like Dawkins.

EVANS. Kevin, I see what you're saying, but if virtually every educated and trained scientist agrees on something—like the big bang—I think the smarter position is to trust the experts.

MILLER. But if God were real, and He really were omnipotent, then wouldn't it be smarter to put our faith and trust in Him and what He says rather than what men, even really intelligent men, say? If God was there and He created the universe and He says He did it in six days, wouldn't that be more authoritative than what some of our colleagues—who were not there—theorize about? Wouldn't God be the real expert on that?

EVANS. Well, come on…

MILLER. And the big bang. Doesn't that theory essentially require us to believe that everything came from nothing? Is that easier to believe than that a higher being—God—created it all?

EVANS. You have gone pretty deep on this, haven't you?

MILLER. I want… I need…to know the truth.

EVANS. I get it. But there are a lot of enormous *ifs* in what you're saying.

MILLER. I recognize that.

EVANS. And we could probably go back and forth for days. Speaking of which, what time…(*Evans looks at his watch.*) Oh no! I'd better run! (*Evans puts his glass down and runs for his hat and coat.*)

MILLER. Now?

EVANS. Sorry, Kevin. Rain check on the chess game…and the debate?

MILLER, *disappointed.* Sure.

Evans stops at the door and faces Miller.

EVANS. Merry Christmas, Kevin. Let me know what you think of that almond-cake thing. (*Evans shudders and makes a disgusted face.*)

MILLER, *opening the door for Evans with a half-smile.* Give Helen my love.

Evans claps him on the shoulder and dashes out the door.

MILLER. Run, little elf, run!

Miller closes the door and stands contemplatively for a moment. Then he takes his cell phone from his pocket and calls a number.

MILLER. Hello, Hope? Yes, it is... I'm doing pretty well, thank you... I wanted to call to let you know that if it's still okay... I will be joining you for Christmas dinner tomorrow. Yes...well, thank you for the invitation. Hey, you left your Bible here yesterday... No, it's not a problem. Actually, I've been reading it. Is that okay? I can bring it back to you tomorrow... Oh, I couldn't do that. I can buy one... But it has all these handwritten notes and highlights. You must have had it for years... Well, if you insist... I'm overwhelmed. Thank you... Okay...

(*Miller hangs up the phone, and again stands contemplatively for a moment, then slaps himself on the forehead.*)

MILLER. Knucklehead! I should have asked what I could bring. Oh wait, I know—almond-flour cake!

Miller laughs to himself and crosses to the table where he put the Roosevelt book. He picks it up and runs his fingers along the spine. He opens the book and flips a couple of pages. Then he looks back over to the Bible on the side table. He closes the Roosevelt book and puts it on a shelf. Then he walks over and picks up the Bible.

MILLER. Well, Mr. Bible, you are my second Christmas present this year. Since it's Christmas Eve, maybe we should skip ahead and read a Christmas story. (*Miller flips to the New Testament and starts scanning pages.*) Oh, here we go. "At that time, the Roman emperor, Augustus,"—now he was definitely a real guy—"decreed that a census should be taken throughout the Roman

Empire. This was the first census taken when Quirinius was governor of Syria."

Miller sits on the sofa as he continues reading.

MILLER. "All returned to their own ancestral towns to register for this census. And because Joseph was a descendant of King David, he had to go to Bethlehem in Judea, David's ancient home. He traveled there from the village of Nazareth in Galilee. He took with him Mary, his fiancée, who was now obviously pregnant. And while they were there, the time came for her baby to be born. She gave birth to her first child, a son. She wrapped him snugly in strips of cloth and laid him in a manger, because there was no lodging available for them."

(*Blackout*)

(*End of scene*)

SCENE 2

Setting: Setting: *Miller's living room. Late afternoon. The little Christmas tree from Evans is on the side table, lit up.*

At rise: *Miller is pacing the floor and dictating. Weaver is typing.*

MILLER. Following his victory at Alexandria, and the suicides of Antony and Cleopatra, Octavian was the unchallenged master of the Roman Empire. Though he was technically co-consul with Marcus Agrippa, Octavian ruled Rome as a dictator. However, through a somewhat slavish Roman preference for form and protocol over substance, Octavian and the senate continued to observe the rituals of traditional Roman government. In 27 BC, Octavian was bestowed and adopted the new name Augustus, which can be loosely translated as "the Illustrious One." This new name implied a deification of the emperor and gave him religious as well as political authority... Hope?

WEAVER, *stops and looks up.* Yes, sir?

MILLER. The Romans had a sophisticated, advanced civilization. They also had a well-developed theology and a pantheon of gods and goddesses that they sincerely believed in. How can we be sure that all those Romans, some of whom were pretty smart, were wrong, and that the God of the Bible is the one true God? For that matter, how do we know the Muslims aren't right? Or the Hindus?

WEAVER. Should I be typing this?

MILLER. No, I'm asking you.

Weaver stops typing and pushes herself away from the stenographic machine.

WEAVER. You sure can ask some big questions, Dr. Miller.

MILLER. Sorry.

WEAVER. I am not a theologian or a Bible teacher. But I will share what I know. In the end, I think the answer to your question once again comes down to faith. I know Jesus is my Lord because I believe what the Bible says about Him and what He said about Himself. But I think other evidence supports it as well. Let's take those Romans. Where is Jupiter now? If Jupiter were really a god, wouldn't he be shouting for us to still worship him? But he's not. He's as quiet as Caesar himself, even though nobody has worshipped him in two thousand years. On the other hand, the worship of the one true God goes back to the Garden of Eden and still goes on to this day in churches all over the world. And no wonder. The gospels contain eyewitness accounts of miracles of every kind performed by Jesus. They also include His declaration that He is God. Jesus proved His divinity by these miracles and by rising from the dead on the third day after He was crucified. That's more than good enough for me.

MILLER. You seem to rely a lot on the Bible to make your argument. How are you so confident in believing that the Bible itself is true?

WEAVER, *smiles.* We could write another whole book on that subject. I know that the Bible is historically accurate, and I think you, as a historian, recognize that now. The Bible also has amazing scientific facts that human scientists didn't figure out until thousands of years later, like how the earth is round, not flat.

MILLER. Yeah, I read Job last night and saw some of that. I really liked the description of the dinosaur.

WEAVER. That's a good one too. Archaeology also supports the truth of the Bible.

MILLER. I did see some of that in my research.

WEAVER. Plus, think about this. The Bible is a collection of sixty-six books written by forty different authors over a span of thousands of years, yet it hangs together as one single story about Jesus Christ and His plan for our salvation. Even right at the beginning, after Adam and Eve ate the forbidden fruit in Genesis, God prophesied that Christ would overcome the serpent—and sin—once and for all. And why do all those different books hang together in harmony? Well, because they were all inspired by the same God—the one true God, of course.

MILLER. But aren't there contradictions in the Bible?

WEAVER. Only superficially. If you read the whole Bible in context, all those contradictions you thought you saw harmonize beautifully. What did you have in mind?

MILLER. For example, in the story of Noah in Genesis, it says that God was sorry He had made humans. If He is omniscient, how could He make a mistake that He could be sorry for?

WEAVER. No, God doesn't make mistakes. Ever. I think that passage means that God was sorry about what He was going to have to do to His creation because of man's sin, not that He wished He had never created the world. The fact that, instead of wiping us out completely, He kept Noah and his family and two of every kind of animal alive shows that He didn't regret His creation, just what sin had done to it.

MILLER. Well…aren't there also contradictions in the four Gospels? They don't all the say the same things, do they?

WEAVER. There are definitely some differences among the Gospels. Some events are not recorded in all four Gospels, for example. But the essential truth is the same, and you have to remember that each Gospel writer was telling the story of Jesus from a unique vantage point and for a distinct purpose. In fact, John even tells us in his Gospel that he is only writing a small fraction of what Jesus did and that what was written was for a specific purpose—so that we might believe that Jesus is the Christ, the Son of God.

MILLER. I see. Do you mind if I ask another question?

WEAVER, *smiling*. I don't mind as long as it's easier than the last couple.

MILLER. In the Gospel of John, Jesus said that He is the Way, the Truth, and the Life and that no man could come to the Father except through Him. Does that mean that everyone who is not a follower of Jesus is going to go to hell?

WEAVER. Yes, I'm afraid it does. We are all sinners. As I've said before, we have all broken God's law, and the punishment for that is hell. The only way to avoid that fate is to repent of our sins and accept the grace of God through Jesus Christ.

MILLER. But what about people on remote islands that have never even heard of Jesus?

WEAVER. All people are accountable to God for their sins. The Bible teaches us that God has revealed Himself to all men in nature and that the heavens declare the glory of God. He has also revealed Himself in the very hearts of men. It is man who refuses to see and refuses to believe. The real answer to your concern is missionary work. Jesus instructed us to take the Gospel to all the world so that all people could hear it and come to Him.

MILLER. But people are dying in those countries every day, right now, without ever hearing about Jesus.

WEAVER. That's why missionary work and evangelism are so critical and so urgent.

MILLER. Wow... Well, what about babies? What if a baby dies? They're too young to know about Jesus.

WEAVER. I think most Christians believe God extends His grace to babies and to small children who are too young to understand their own sin or the Gospel message. Lots of smart Bible teachers have debated on this issue, but I like the story of King David. After the baby he had with Bathsheba died, David said that he would one day go to the child. I think that means he knew his baby was in heaven.

MILLER. Hope, I am sorry to bombard you with all these questions. I know they are hard. I'm really trying to understand. Trying... to believe.

WEAVER. You can pray to Him and ask him to help you in your unbelief. And you continue your study (*smiles*). I can tell you've been busy.

MILLER. I have. I have always been a good student and a quick learner. Hope... I want to thank you again for the amazing gift of your Bible. I read it almost constantly through the holiday weekend.

WEAVER. I am so happy to hear that. You are most welcome. I believe the Lord wanted you to have it.

MILLER. I also want to thank you again for dinner on Christmas. I haven't had a family Christmas in years. I really appreciated it.

WEAVER. We were thrilled to have you. I was so happy you came. I was pretty sure you wouldn't.

MILLER. So was I.

WEAVER. Dr. Miller…

MILLER. Please call me Kevin.

WEAVER. Okay. Kevin…that's going to take some getting used to. Kevin, if you don't mind me saying, you have changed in these last few weeks.

MILLER. Funny, I feel it too. I feel less like I'm living in my own head all the time. I guess thinking about one's mortality can have that effect. I don't even feel the same burning urgency to work on the book. In fact, why don't we knock off for today?

WEAVER. Are you okay? Are you tired? It's not four yet.

MILLER. I think I'd like to go out for a walk and enjoy this beautiful afternoon. Who knows, maybe I'll see God in some of that nature out there like you said.

WEAVER. He's there. I hope you find Him.

MILLER. Me too.

(*Blackout*)

(*End of scene*)

SCENE 3

Setting: *Miller's living room at night.*

At rise: *Miller is sitting at the table editing some of the many papers stacked on the table. The room is dark except for Miller and the area around him. A bottle of prescription medicine is also on the table.*

Miller rapidly flips through and scans several pages while muttering under his breath. He stops on a particular page and holds it up to study it.

MILLER. Frederick I became king of Prussia upon the death of his father in 1740... That's not right. (*Miller begins striking out words on the paper and writing in new text.*) It was Frederick II, not Frederick I. And he wasn't king *of* Prussia yet in 1740. He was king *in* Prussia. He didn't become king *of* Prussia until 1772...

Miller smacks himself lightly on the head.

MILLER. Come on, Miller, you know better than that. Wake up. You're never going to finish this if...(*Miller puts his pen down and starts rubbing his eyes and face.*) So tired. I'm just so tired. (*Miller picks up the prescription bottle and swallows a pill. Then he resumes his editing.*) Wait...this part about the First Silesian War is wrong too.

Miller puts the paper and pen down again and pushes them away. He pushes himself away from the table and puts his face in his hands. Moments later, he raises his hands toward the ceiling and looks up.

MILLER. Why? Why are you doing this to me? Why me? (*Miller begins to sob. He collects himself and looks up.*) Why does it have to hurt so bad? I can't eat. I can't sleep. I can't even think any more! At least leave me that. Please leave me that…

Miller begins to sob again. Then his pain turns to anger. He pulls himself to his feet.

MILLER. Answer me! Don't I at least deserve an answer? Why me? (*Miller pushes the piles of transcripts off the table in anger.*) Are you even there? Are you listening? Do you even care? Why me? Why do I have to die? God of love, huh? Then why…why don't you love me?

Miller sobs again. He has an obviously painful coughing fit and slowly regains his composure. He slumps back in to the chair.

MILLER. I don't want to die. I don't want…

Miller hangs his head a moment as if in deep thought. Then he rises and starts picking papers off the floor and putting them back on the table. He sits down and begins sorting them back into piles.

MILLER. Am I even supposed to finish this? Does it even matter? (*Miller stops sorting, puts the papers down, and looks up.*) Couldn't you just heal me? You healed the lepers. You made the blind see. You raised Lazarus from the dead!

Miller resumes his sorting. He has another short coughing fit and wipes away a tear.

MILLER. Maybe it could just hurt less? Maybe I could just sleep at night? (*Miller resumes sorting. He stops abruptly and looks up.*) What do you want from me? What more do I have left?

Miller returns to the papers, looking for a specific page. He finds the page he had been editing and holds it up.

MILLER. Where was I? (*Miller resumes editing.*) I'll move this here...

Miller stops writing and puts his pen down. He sits quietly a moment, then rises, moves to the end table, and picks up his Bible. He returns to the table and sits. He opens the Bible and flips through it as if searching for a specific passage. He stops at Job 38:1 and begins reading out loud.

MILLER. Then the Lord answered Job from the whirlwind: Who is this that questions my wisdom with such ignorant words? Brace yourself like a man because I have some questions for you, and you must answer them. Where were you when I laid the foundations of the earth? Tell me, if you know so much. Who determined its dimensions and stretched out the surveying line? What supports its foundations, and who laid its cornerstone as the morning stars sang together and all the angels shouted for joy?

MILLER, *stops reading, closes his eyes and looks up again.* Please help me. Please help me to believe. Please tell me it is not too late. (*Miller folds his arms on the table and rests his head on them.*) Please...

(*Blackout*)

(*End of scene*)

SCENE 4

Setting: *Miller's living room. Morning. It is now spring.*

At rise: *Miller is dictating and Weaver is typing. The stacks of transcripts are getting quite high. Unlike prior scenes, Miller is dictating while sitting instead of pacing. He is wrapped in a blanket and shivers. Weaver has exchanged her usual sweaters and long sleeves for a bright spring dress.*

Miller's speech is slow and interrupted by frequent coughs.

MILLER. The Jacobite uprising met its end at the Battle of Culloden Moor on April...16, 1745. Bonnie Prince Charlie's ragtag army...was savaged by the better-trained...better-equipped and better-led army of the Duke of Cumberland—(*abruptly and with an air of finality*). That's enough, Hope. I don't need to work on the book anymore...

WEAVER, *looks up.* Are you okay? You look feverish. (*Weaver gets up, walks over and touches Miller's forehead.*) You're burning up! Come and lie down.

Weaver helps Miller up and to the sofa. She covers him with the blanket.

WEAVER. Do you have something you can take for fever? Can I get you anything? Should I call your doctor?

MILLER. Just some water, please.

Weaver pours him a glass of water and brings it to him.

WEAVER. Are you sure I can't bring you anything else?

MILLER. Please help me sit up. It's too hard to breathe lying down.

Weaver helps him sit up. Miller takes a long drink of water, then has a bad coughing fit, though the coughs are weaker.

WEAVER. I really think I should call someone…

MILLER, *closing his eyes*. Just so tired. I'll be okay…

WEAVER. You rest. We can worry about the book when you're feeling better. But maybe I should go ahead and just check in with your doctor.

Weaver goes to her bag and retrieves her phone. She moves to the side table, picks up a business card and calls the number on it.

WEAVER. Hello. Yes, my name is Hope Weaver. I am here with Dr. Kevin Miller, who is Dr. Jackson's patient… Well, he seems to be running a very high fever and is coughing even worse than usual… No, I'm sorry. I haven't checked it… A nurse? Is Dr. Jackson available? Okay, then… Hello… Is this Dr. Jackson's nurse? I'm with Dr. Kevin Miller, and he seems very sick… I'm a friend… Well, he's very warm. I think it's a high fever, but I'm sorry, I haven't checked it, and he's coughing worse than I've ever seen him… Hospital? How long? Okay, thank you very much. Goodbye. (*She hangs up the phone.*) Dr. Miller, they are sending an ambulance to take you to the hospital. They should be here in a few minutes. Is there anything you'd like me to pack to bring with us?

Miller, *without opening his eyes*. Our Bible…and my robe. I hate those hospital gowns…all open in the back… They should let a man keep at least a little dignity.

Weaver retrieves a robe from offstage and puts it and the Bible in her own bag.

WEAVER. Anything else?

MILLER. Hope, I need to know something.

WEAVER. What is that? (*Weaver sits beside Miller and takes his hand.*)

MILLER, *opens his eyes and looks solemnly at her.* I have read the Bible all the way through twice. I have continued to study it every day. I have listened to sermons. And I've done research to find answers to things I didn't…understand. But there's one thing… I still just can't answer.

WEAVER. What is that?

MILLER. If God loves us, and He is all good and all powerful, why does He permit suffering and pain? Why does He let bad things—terrible things—happen to good people? (*He swallows hard.*) If He loves me…why did He let me get cancer?

WEAVER. He is most certainly all good and all powerful. And He knows everything that has happened, everything that is happening, and everything that will happen. He knows and commands everything so completely that we can't possibly understand His eternal perspective. But because we know He is good, we can trust that even when we can't see how something could possibly work out for good, He is in control. He's got this. And yes, Dr. Miller, He most certainly loves you. I can't claim to see or understand all of His reasons, but answer me this—if you hadn't gotten cancer, would we be having this conversation? Would you be reading and studying the Bible or doing theological research? Ask yourself, Would you rather live another forty years in blissful ignorance and spend eternity in hell or have the Lord use something terrible like cancer to get your attention?

He loves you so much He died for you. Maybe…maybe He loves you so much He let you get sick.

MILLER. I want to know the truth. (*Miller grabs Weaver's arm and looks in her eyes.*) Are you sure it's not too late for me? I have sinned so many times, and I have denied and mocked Him for so long…

WEAVER. It is never too late. You're close, Dr. Miller. So close. He's waiting for you with open arms. Confess your sins to Him. Beg His forgiveness. Make Him your Lord and accept His salvation.

Miller begins weeping. Weaver takes both his hands.

MILLER. I don't… I don't know what to say.

WEAVER. Just tell Him what you feel in your heart.

MILLER. Jesus, I'm so sorry… I didn't know…please forgive me. Thank you for dying for my sins. Please save me. Thank you for not abandoning me. Thank you for showing me…

WEAVER, *looking heavenward.* Thank you, dear Lord.

MILLER. Thank you, Lord Jesus… Thank you…(*A sudden moment of recognition.*) Hope, I was wrong. There's one more entry I have to make in the book.

WEAVER. Right now?

MILLER, *insistent.* Please… Brian…he doesn't believe. But he said he'd read the book… He has to know…

WEAVER. Yes. Of course. Please don't get agitated. It will make you cough. (*Weaver goes to her stenographic machine and gets ready to type.*) I'm ready.

Miller clears his throat and begins. He musters the last of his strength so he can speak boldly. Weaver types as he speaks.

MILLER. *Everything I Know.* Final entry… Jesus Christ is my Lord and Savior. Kevin Miller is going to heaven.

Miller exhales and smiles as tears stream down his cheeks.

WEAVER, *through tears.* Amen, Father. Amen. Thank you, Lord…

MILLER. I just need to sleep now…

Miller lies down on the sofa. He is smiling as he closes his eyes. Weaver gets up and covers him up with the blanket. She notices his face has gone limp. She checks, and he's not breathing anymore.

WEAVER. Dr. Miller! Kevin! (*A pause as Weaver wipes away tears. She puts her hand on his head.*) Say hello to Jesus for me, okay?

A loud knock on the door. Weaver calmly goes to the door and opens it. Two paramedics enter, carrying equipment.

FIRST PARAMEDIC. Is this Dr. Miller's home?

WEAVER. Yes.

SECOND PARAMEDIC, *looking around the room.* Where is the patient?

WEAVER. You won't find him here. (*Weaver smiles.*) Dr. Kevin Miller is in heaven.

(*Blackout*)

(*End of scene*)

SCENE 5

Setting: *Miller's living room. The day after Miller's funeral.*

At rise: *Evans is taking books off the bookshelf and putting them in boxes. The shelves are mostly empty. There are a number of full and empty boxes scattered about the room.*

EVANS, *admiring one of the books.* Quite a nice little collection you've got here, Kevin. No wonder you're so…smart. (*Evans hangs his head briefly, clears his throat, and resumes boxing the books.*)

WEAVER, *appears in the open doorway. She is carrying an upholstered bag. She watches Evans a moment, then knocks on the open door.* Dr. Evans, my name is Hope. I met you briefly at the memorial service. I'm sorry to intrude, but your wife told me I'd find you here.

Evans, *startled, stops and looks at Weaver.* Yes. Yes. Hope. (*Evans begins walking to Weaver.*) Please come in. I'm sorry there isn't really a place to sit down. I'm boxing Kevin's things, and I'm afraid I've made a mess. (*Evans shakes hands with Weaver, and they move into the room.*) What can I do for you?

WEAVER. Dr. Evans, I—

EVANS. Brian, please.

WEAVER. Brian, I… I didn't know Dr. Miller nearly as long or as well as you did, but he was very dear to me.

69

EVANS. Best friend I ever had.

WEAVER. I wanted to tell you that your eulogy was lovely. It was obvious how much you loved him. He loved you too.

Evans wipes tears from his eyes and clears his throat.

WEAVER. I have some things that I know Dr. Miller wanted you to have.

EVANS. For me?

Weaver reaches into her bag and produces a flash drive. She hands it to Evans.

EVANS. What is…?

WEAVER. This is Dr. Miller's book, *Everything I Know*. He used to say you were the only person who was ever going to read it.

EVANS. I will. I will. Thank you.

WEAVER. Dr. Miller made his final entry just for you. In his last moments, he wanted you to know the truth that he had found.

EVANS. Truth?

WEAVER. The truth. That he needed—that we all need—a Savior. (*Weaver reaches into her bag and produces Miller's Bible.*) That's how I know he wanted you to have this too. (*She hands the Bible to Evans.*)

EVANS. A Bible? Your Bible?

WEAVER. Dr. Miller's Bible. I know he read it every day. It led him to Jesus.

EVANS. Hope, I'm grateful that you cared so much for Kevin. I'm very grateful for the comfort that you brought him. I'm even grateful that you would think he'd want me to have something that was important to him. But I'm not really a believer in all that. (*Evans gestures with the Bible.*)

WEAVER, *smiling.* Neither was Dr. Miller until he started reading God's Word. Now he's with Jesus in eternity.

EVANS, *seriously, not mocking.* Do you really believe Kevin is in heaven?

WEAVER, *smiling.* With every fiber of my being!

EVANS, *choking up.* I'd like that. I wish I could believe that.

WEAVER, *kindly.* You can, Brian. You can. It's all in here. (*Weaver touches the Bible in Evans's hands.*) Now I should be getting on and let you finish up here. I need to get home and get busy in the kitchen. My son is visiting today, and if I don't have his favorite meatloaf ready for him, there will be trouble! (*Weaver walks to the door and turns to look at Evans.*) Think about it some more, Dr. Evans. Then you can call me if you want to talk about it. I put my card in the Bible. Take care. (*Weaver turns and leaves.*)

Evans, *quietly, and to the empty door.* Goodbye…

Evans looks at the Bible, shrugs his shoulders, then tosses it into an open box. He resumes taking books off the shelf and putting them into an empty box. After two handfuls of books, he comes upon African Game Trails, *the book he gave Miller for Christmas. He looks the book over and runs his hand over the cover.*

EVANS. *African Game Trails.* (*Evans opens the book and stops on the signed title page.*) Theodore Roosevelt…(*Evans clutches the book to his chest and begins to cry.*) Oh, Kevin... Kevin... I'm so sorry...so...

Evans cries again. He slowly recovers, takes a handkerchief out of his pocket, and dries his eyes. He hangs his head a moment, puts the book he is holding back on the shelf, then moves back to the box with the Bible in it. He retrieves the Bible and puts it on the table. He takes a box off one of the chairs and sits down at the table. He looks the Bible over, flips through it, then opens it to the book of Genesis and begins to read out loud.

EVANS. In the beginning, God created the heavens and the earth...

(*Blackout*)

(*End of play*)

QUESTIONS FOR CONTEMPLATION AND DISCUSSION

1. What motivated Hope to leave her Bible with Dr. Miller?

2. What made Dr. Miller receptive to the Gospel message?

3. Why did Evans begin reading the Bible in the final scene?

4. What character trait of Hope stands out most to you?

5. Think of a person you know who does not know the Lord. Have you shared the Gospel with this person? If not, why not?

6. Are there steps you could take to share the Gospel with the unsaved people in your daily life?

7. Hope shares the Gospel with someone she is working for. Why is it so difficult to share the Gospel with someone we encounter in our work?

8. Do you know someone who is suffering from a terminal disease? Does this person know the Lord? How does whether a person knows the Lord impact his/her ability to cope with such a medical condition?

9. Hope does not have a seminary degree or any college education at all. How is she equipped to share the Gospel?

10. Studying the Bible is a central theme of *Everything I Know*. Do you study the Bible regularly? If not, what are you spending time on that you could replace with Bible reading?